Pets Only

Pets Only

Shadow Tang

Library of Congress Control Number: 2012903020
ISBN: Hardcover   978-1-4691-7019-0
               Softcover   978-1-4691-7018-3
               Ebook   978-1-4691-7020-6

To order additional copies of this book, contact:
Xlibris Corporation
1-888-795-4274
www.Xlibris.com
Orders@Xlibris.com
99099

DEDICATED TO MOM, WE MISS YOU SO MUCH

Credits

Contributors

Hassan "C-10" and Becky Chehaitelli
Jennifer, Julian, Zachary, Katherine and Jackson Kassner
Raymond Rahman Moshe
CDR Leonard V. "Rip" Rohrer, USN (Ret.)
COL Ronald Roughead, USA (Ret.)
Dana Lynne Tang (Mom)
Kimberly F. Tang
Lilly H, Tang
Tom W. H. Tang

In Memoriam

Bogee
Champion
Emily
Godfrey
Loki
Lucy
Mao Mi
Matilda (Matti)
Sheba
Sushi

Author's Note

Events chronicled in this book were based on personal experience and anecdotes collected from friends, colleagues and other acquaintances. Names, dates, times and places were altered to protect the guilty. If you thought you were one of the subjects portrayed within, well, you "could" be right.

Have a flea free day. Woof, woof.

Shadow Tang

CHAPTER 1

The Pack

Self-portrait

Woof; I'm Shadow, a purebred black Labrador Retriever, and I live at #1 Dana Lynne Lane, off Route 612 in Stafford, Virginia. According to Mom and

Dad, they'd thought long and hard about my naming before they settled on "Shadow," not due to the color of my hair, but because on the first day of my arrival at home, I followed Mom everywhere she went, like I was her shadow.

My first day/evening with Mom, being her shadow.

THE PACK

We are a typical American family, a melting pot of all sorts and breeds. Dad's from China, the proud product of over five thousand years of genetic amalgamations involving northern, southern and western barbarians that fought and lived in that East Asian land. Mom's a Navy brat of Iowa farm stock with doses of Vikings, Scots, French and German in her genetic heritage, accounting for her reddish blond hair and emerald green eyes. Had she been a little taller, she could have been a double for Maureen O'Hara, Dad's favorite movie starlet. Mom's maternal grandmother claimed to have crossed the American Great Plains in a Conestoga and had met Geronimo along the way. By the way, just who the heck was this Geronimo cat? He sounded like a mean junkyard mongrel.

In a moment of levity, Dad pompously proclaimed possessively to Mom, "You are my trophy wife."

"In that case, you are my laundry service, houseboy and cook." Back came the immediate retort.

Undaunted, Dad persisted, "I brought home the bacon; therefore, I am the ruler of the roost."

Just as he was turning away, Mom slipped in a last quip, "And you have my permission to say so publicly." For once, Dad was left without a word. So, I leave you to guess who was the one really in charge? My vote went to Mom; woof, woof.

All kidding aside, I knew they got along well and loved each other so very much. The secret for their lasting relationship—all sins of the day were forgotten at the stroke of midnight, no grudges were to be held beyond the witching hour. Personally, I thought Grandpa Ye Ye's (Dad's Dad) approval of Mom tipped the scale in her favor, because no self-respecting Chinese would dare to incur the wrath of his esteem father.

However, you should know that within the pack, Dad laid down the rules, and everyone followed. A slight throaty growl expelled through his nose issued a warning that immediately got our attention. Mom referred to it as "Dad's noise," which worked like magic in maintaining pack discipline. He'd communicate with us in direct single syllable words—a short and easy to understand sentence; the tone of his voice conveyed the sense of urgency he demanded. Did you know that Chinese was a tonal language? When he barked your name in that sharp nasal Chinglish (Chinese-English) twang you knew you were in deep doodle.

However, Dad never punished us with his hand, it was reserved for strokes and praises; instead, a rolled up newspaper became the standard implement for discipline. It didn't hurt, but sure made a lot of scary noises. You didn't try to run, because his order of "stay" glued your paws in place until you were released from the command by a snap of his fingers. When each person joined the pack, Dad always initiated him or her to his remote control devices—slippers and shoes; they were the reasons that we didn't play with footwear—we associated them with punishment.

Speaking of punishments, the worst offender of pack rules, whatever they were, got dispatched into solitary

THE PACK

confinement, better known as "The Cooler"—namely a large portable cage at the front porch, which Mom referred to as "The Jail." When Dad or Mom said "Go to Jail," you just pinned your ears back, clamped your tail between your hind legs and wiggled-waggled in to the pen—and then stayed in. The jail door was never locked, but you knew better than to come out without permission. Sometimes, when we boo-booed, we would check ourselves into "The Cooler." The voluntary guilty plea saved on mental stress to all parties concerned, with the added incentive of a possibly reduced sentence for the culprit. By the way, the Cooler only applied to us canines; I never saw any other specie sentenced there for punishment, certainly not any of the other furred, finned, nor feathered members of the clan. I thought that was canine discrimination, but who could I complain to, the ASPCA?

To accommodate the whole pack and the frequent visitors, Mom and Dad bought forty some acres of woodland in northern Virginia and built a home of their own design. The driveway was longer than most streets, thirteen hundred feet to be exact, and Dad named it after Mom—Dana Lynne Lane, so that was how our house number came into being.

Dad liked to cook and entertain. He thought a restaurant at the front portion of the new home was a good idea. Well aware of Mom's predisposition toward animals, Dad slyly approached the scheme by suggesting that they make it a pet-friendly establishment with the name of "Pets Only." Human customers must be accompanied by a pet or pets—that is to say, **No Pets, No Service.** The stratagem succeeded and Mom gave her blessing, thus Pets Only came into existence.

Of course, the guests' pets had to behave with proper social etiquette, or they would be ejected with their masters in tow, and that was why Loki got installed as the maître de. Her friendly disposition was tailor made for the job. Of course, guess who got to be the bouncer. Gurr!

Mom and Loki

THE PACK

Loki, the grand dame of the pack, was an F2 Wolf/Collie mix—a beautiful lady with a long white and gold sable coat and green eyes that matched those of Mom's. Loki greeted the customers then led them to their stalls. The wolfie wiles of her sharp mind helped determine the social acceptability of the patrons. For the convenience of the occasional pet-deprived human customers, we rented or sold bowls of beautiful guppies and betas to those people so that they could comply with the house rule regarding pet companionship. With no competition within ten miles, Pets Only became the favorite watering hole of the neighborhood. It was a neat sight to see all sorts of exotic walkers, crawlers and flyer friends as they came for visits with their humans in tow; believe it or not, some humans even brought their swimmer friends to Pets Only.

One desperate biker patron looped a chain around his lady friend and claimed her to be his pet to satisfy the house rule regarding pets. Personally, in view of the man's bodily fur, I thought he should be the one wearing the chain, as he fitted the mold of a pet better than his lady friend. But, since he was the paying customer, I kept my opinion to myself.

Pet's Only had a very simple menu for human patrons: Chinese chicken pot stickers (dumplings), fried rice (for some reason Dad called it 'flied lice'), Shawarma (a mid-Eastern chicken/lamb wrap), and a "Chinese supplise," all to be washed down with a wide assortment of beverages. The "Chinese supplise" was whatever dish Dad felt like making on that particular day; it was not necessarily a Chinese cuisine, just something cooked up by Dad—a Chinese chef. Dad shared the chef duties with Grandma Mah Mah and Hassan, a tall and handsome Lebanese who handled the Shawarma. The food was great and the sauces were just out of this world: trust me, one sniff and you were in heaven. If you wanted to sample some you had to pay for them; meanwhile, I got them without even having to beg.

On the other paw, we maintained a very extensive side menu for the 'primary' customers, it entailed several brand named wet and dry foodstuff, corn, hay, oats, plus a variety of dried fruits, grains, nuts and seeds for the discriminating taste of our guests. Should a human customer be really particular, we allowed them to BYOB (Bring Your Own Bag—Doggie Bag) to be consumed on the premises (by the 'pets' only of course, no sharing allowed).

Despite the immense size of the inn, seating at the restaurant was limited because we maintained several large partitioned seating booths for guests with exotic requirements; some special compartments were set apart to accommodate XXX sized patrons, such as donkeys, ponies, horses, llamas, alpacas, Jabbas . . . etc. Those stalls had large open grassy areas with hitching posts, this way guests and their companions could dine together in close (to each other) comfort. Oh, by the way, we kept shovels and wheelbarrows on hand for occasional special needs. It was the responsibility of the human patrons to clean up after their companions, and sometimes themselves. Of course, we had some segregated seating for human customers with allergies (to pets); they (the pet challenged humans) were the ones that usually rented guppies or betas.

Grandpa Ye Ye & Grandma Mah Mah (file photo)

Grandpa Ye Ye was an accountant, thus he became the natural choice as the keeper of the till. Chinese were renowned for their frugality, and Grandpa Ye Ye's ancestors would have been exceptionally proud of their scion. His penny pinching habits easily put Ebenezer Scrooge to shame. Once in a while, you could see him patching plastic grocery shopping bags with scotch tape, so that they could be reused. Even Dad rolled his eyes on that one, woof woof. Another time, he suggested washing paper plates so that they could be reused. However, the piece-de-resistance was when he had a gaping hole in his shoes. He refused to buy a new pair; instead, he sought to duct tape the footwear for continued use. That was when Grandma Mah Mah (Dad's Mom) stepped in, threw the hole-ly shoe into the dumpster, thus forcing Grandpa Ye Ye to buy a new pair of shoes. But, one should never mistake frugality for miserliness. Grandpa enjoyed dining and considered it as his right, privilege and responsibility, as the elder of the clan to paw the bill when we ate out. But I digress; let me get back to the subject at paw—our Inn.

Grandma Mah Mah was a kindly and intelligent lady. With no basic elementary school education, she managed to be fluent in four dialects of Chinese, plus Japanese, English, and a smattering of French, Spanish and Dog Speak. In addition, she was an accomplished chef, which meant she ran the kitchen in the Inn. Of course everyone loved her, if you liked good tasty food that is. By the way, she was the one that taught Dad everything he knew about cooking, and everyone considered Dad as an excellent chef.

However, on the lighter side, Grandma Mah Mah often got western names mixed up. Case in point, Osama bin Laden, the notorious leader of the terrorist al Qaeda organization became Osama Dean Martin; Mitt Romney, the Republican Presidential candidate became Mickey Rooney; finally, A well known Japanese Tsunami restaurant became the Salami restaurant. Woof, woof, :-P. However, she never had any problem with our names, so we didn't really care how she masticated those people's titles. The important point being, she fed me well, which was the only thing that counted in my book.

CHAPTER 2

Auntie Sheba's Wedding

Auntie Sheba

One warm summer afternoon, a shiny black Lexus SUV raised a cloud of dust as it zipped up our driveway, and out popped two dogs—a chubby tan and black Pug, and a black pure bred mutt. A man and a woman followed the visitors out of the SUV. The woman dangled a cat carrier in one hand, as she waved to us with the other. Loki barked joyfully, wagged her tail vigorously like a windmill and ran up to greet our visitors and the humans. She rubbed her side against the woman's left leg; and the human female bent down to set the cat carrier on the ground then gave Loki a loving bear hug, while enduring a spate of energetic licking in return.

Next thing I knew, a black streak flashed past me to jump into the mix, knocking the woman onto the gravel. Between dodging slobbering kisses, the woman laughed and cried, "OK, OK, I love you too Sheba," as she let go of Loki to clasp the very excited Sheba to her bosom, all the while lying with her back on the ground.

As I walked up to get in on the action, an unexpected wave of apprehension and trepidation crept up toward me from an unexpected quarter. It emanated from the male human that had accompanied the woman. He was tall and swarthy with thick curly hair and heavy brows. I looked up into his face, and saw two large round bulging eyes staring at me behind a pair of thick set eye glasses, setting off alarm bells in my security instinct. I reflexively peeled back my lips to bare my teeth and growled in preparation for defending myself and the pack. The man shrank back a little at my aggressive posture then slowly withdrew into the protection of the car.

Meanwhile, Mom and Dad had heard the noise, and came out to investigate the commotion. Dad barked "Loki, Sheba come!" The command quickly restored order out of chaos, as the two of them reluctantly left the woman's side to sit down next to Dad. That allowed Mom to reach down and help the woman to her feet. "Wow, that was some warm welcome," gasped the woman as she brushed the dirt from her clothes and allowed herself to be hugged and kissed by Mom and Dad in turn.

"Well, Jill this is a surprise. I see you brought your pack," Mom gestured with her hand toward the visitors. So that was Jill, Mom's daughter. I had heard talk of her pending visit, but had never met her before.

Jill swung around as if she was looking for something; then she found it inside her car. She motioned with her hand and said, "Jack, come out of there and meet Mom and Dad." The man glanced at me from the inside of the SUV with uncertainty, shook his head and pointed a long finger of his right hand at me. I wagged my tail back at him in a friendly greeting.

Dad quickly surmised the situation and took in the source of Jack's reservation. He called to me, "Shadow, heel." As I obeyed, he gave another command, "Go home!" and pointed his right hand toward the house. Surprised, I slowly backed away from the group of people, feeling confused by the command. "Humph!" Dad gave his Chinglish nasal grunt, the tone left no room for equivocation. Reluctantly, I sighed and slinked over to the porch of the house; but, that was as far as I would go, this way I could, at the least, still keep an eye on things at the Inn. It was just too doggone unfair. Jack was the one that initiated the challenge; I didn't understand why I should be punished for something that was not my fault. Alas, as they said, "Ours was not to reason why, ours but to bark and fright."

*   *   *

Sheba, the black streak that had knocked Jill on her duff, was our klutzy Auntie, a pure bred Chesapeake Bay Labrador Retriever. Her shiny black coat glowed midnight blue under the moon. Hassan said she must have been a descendent from the beautiful Ethiopian Queen that was her namesake. According to Dad, the original Queen Sheba had seduced King Solomon, a wise King of Israel that had lived a few thousand or so years ago.

Auntie Sheba had a happy-go-lucky personality and the kindest heart you could find. If she had one weakness it would be that she liked to eat, so she leaned slightly on the chubby side of the scale. I mean, everyone liked to eat, but there were limits to gluttony. That was the reason she had no responsibilities at Pets Only. She just could not be trusted with the goods. Besides, it was for her own good not to overfeed her.

"I'm going to a party! I'm going to the wedding!" Sheba barked happily as she pranced merrily up the path and onto the porch.

"What are you yapping about?" I asked her.

"Jack and Jill are getting married, and I'm going to be their bridesmaid."

"And how many pounds you intend to gain from that experience?"

She paused in mid step, then shook her head in a gesture of disregard, "Who cares?" then she danced past me into the living room to spread the good news.

Soon afterwards, I saw Loki came trotting up the path with Jill's two pack mates in tow. Still miffed at the recent mistreatment caused by Jack, I took it out on the two guests. I stood up, glared down at the dogs and growled. The big mutt shrank back to hide behind the short and smaller Pug, who stiffened his fur, then glared with his bulging eyes and growled back at me. I must say, the kid's got spunk. Loki took a step onto the porch and interceded before things got out of paw. "Back off, Shadow; this is Oscar and Beatle Bailey, Jill's pack mates. They are guests, so behave yourself!" When I hesitated, Loki peeled back her lips to expose her canines accompanied by a throaty growl, which was akin to that of Dad's, and I moved aside and lied down so that they could enter the house in peace. Loki moved and stood next to me to let the guests enter first.

I took the opportunity to look up at Loki and inquired, "What's this I heard about Sheba going to a wedding?"

She cocked her head to glance down sideways out of the corner of her eyes, then grinned sagely, "Before you came along, Sheba had been with Jill. She left Sheba with Mom before heading off to nursing school. Now that she had finished her schooling, she would probably want to reclaim Sheba. In fact, the cat Jill brought with her used to live with us also, she's called Pookie, and you should be nice to her. Just remember to be tolerant, because she's got some idiosyncrasies." I flicked my ear and gave Loki a questioning look, but she refused to say anything more on the subject. That was so typical of her, being thoughtful and considerate of other people's short comings.

Mom persuaded Jack and Jill to have their wedding at our Inn; it was probably Dad's idea, to save on expenses for the rental of the Synagogue and festivities; which gave Mom cause to tease Dad by mimicking Bogee the cockatiel, "Cheap cheap cheap." You know how frugal and calculating the Chinese could get. By the way, that must have been the reason their inscrutable ancestors invented the world's first computer, the abacus, to help them with the bean counting.

I supposed it was only right that Jill wanted Auntie Sheba as one of the bridesmaids because Auntie Sheba was Jill's baby. Just as Loki had predicted, now Jill wanted Auntie Sheba back into her (Jill's) life. Of course, my confrontation with Jack did not improve my chances to be on the guest list at Jill's wedding.

Everyone got excited with the preparations for the wedding. As a member of the bridal party, Auntie Sheba got to go to the bachelorette party and the rehearsal dinner. Needless to say, she gained a few extra pounds from those festive experiences. Fortunately for her, all she had to fit into was a floral collar (her neck didn't grow as much as her waistline), and there was no need for a bridesmaid dress for Auntie, thus no size adjustment necessary.

For the ceremony, Auntie Sheba got paired with Ahmed, a short, dark but handsome Egyptian that matched well with her pedigree. I believed Ahmed was the most surprised person at the wedding. He considered himself quite a ladies' man and had relentlessly pestered Jill for information about his partner in the coming ceremony. Mom grinned impishly when she overheard him mutter, "Sheba, what an exotic biblical name! I must get to know her better."

Jill being Jill told Ahmed the truth about Auntie Sheba; not the whole truth, mind you, just part of the truth. By the time she was done, you could see Ahmed panting and drooling to get better acquainted with the beautiful Nubian nymphomaniac from the Eastern Shore of the Chesapeake Bay, who would eagerly leap into the arms of any male, ready to obey his every command. Unfortunately for Ahmed, Auntie Sheba was not present for the rehearsal, and he had missed the rehearsal dinner; so he never got to meet his bridesmaid partner until the ceremony.

I wish I had been there at the wedding, to see Ahmed's face when he Dad handed over Auntie Sheba's leash to her date. Ruff-ha-ha. As told to us by Auntie Sheba, at the reception party after she danced with Dad, she jumped into Ahmed's lap and gave him the best tonguing a man could ever ask for.

Needless to say, part of the wedding cake went inside Auntie Sheba, while a good deal of the stuff ended on and around Ahmed.

That night, the JJ's (Jack and Jill) used our guestroom as their nuptial suite. Unfortunately, they had accidentally closed the door with a third party inside. She happened to be our feisty orange tabby with a very appropriate name of Emily. For the less informed ones, it was a name derived from the Latin word *Aemulus* meaning "Rival." She became a celebrity for a few days because of her feline curiosity.

 AUNTIE SHEBA'S WEDDING

Auntie Sheba the Bridesmaid—A champagne toast with the bride

As we settled into bed for the night, a blood curdling scream chased everyone out of the bed. Loki started barking and searching for the source of the commotion, with the whole pack rumbling behind her. Finally, things calmed down and the truth came to the fore. It appeared that, in the middle of the night, Emily had emerged from her hideout in the closet. Lured by the undulating motion of the bedspread, she decided to jump in and investigate with all twenty-four of her sharp claws; and that was how JJ's marriage got consummated. Ruff, ruff, ha, ha.

By the way, Emily gave her official stamp of approval to the union of the JJ's by leaving her teeth marks on the corner of their marriage certificate. What a Cat! In case you haven't caught on yet, Emily was a Hemingway cat, with six toes on each paw, ergo the twenty-four claws.

The JJ's left for their honeymoon, and we got three house guests for two weeks—Oscar, Beatle Bailey and Pookie, the blue eyed Burmese cat.

*　　　　　*　　　　　*

As I mentioned before, Oscar had what I would call a Napoleon syndrome; small in stature, but with the ego of a Great Dane. Fearless and aggressive, he attacked anything that got in his way. Well, almost anything. He tried to alpha Taz—*big mistake*. A shrinking violet, Taz was not. The day after the JJ's took off for Hawaii, Oscar decided to make his claim for status within the pack. Since Taz was the junior male member of the pack, Oscar had to start with the bottom rung—Taz.

The Pug tried to take a chew hide away from the Boxer, who took immediate and drastic action to put Oscar in his place. Taz charged at Oscar, who stood his ground and growled at the advancing Boxer. Depending on your point of view, it was a beautiful sight to see Oscar doing stunt double duty for Superdog. The Pug got bowled over like a tenpin in a bowling alley; and presto! Taz invented 'Pug Bowling.'

Oscar tumbled through the air, bounced on the ground a couple of times then rolled down the slope. Of course, he quickly flipped over onto his feet and charged at Taz, but the poor Pug was panting and wheezing before he even got back halfway up the hill. Taz's long legs easily out distanced the gasping shorty. In fact, being the playful kid that he was, Taz ran a few circles around the Pug then stopped to challenge him to a race. I'll say one thing for Oscar, that Pug had pluck. He charged and charged, but it was like chasing your own tail—an exercise in futility. When he got tired and stopped to gasp for air, Taz would be right there in his face to tease him for another round of tag. By then, I couldn't resist the urge to charge full tilt into the fray, knocking both Taz and Oscar tumbling down the slope. Subsequently, the situation degenerated into a scrum, with everybody fighting for himself; aah, so exhilarating. The fact that Taz also got beat up gave the Pug some semblance of revenge and face saving grace. Besides, he was too spent to complaint about the entire incident; not to mention the fact that he was the instigator of the ruckus, when he tried to take away Taz's chew hide. I felt the deed killed two birds with one bone; it settled the pecking order dispute and, at the same time, reinforced my status within the pack.

Beatle Bailey took a cue from Oscar's experience and did not even make an attempt at asserting himself in front of us. Nevertheless, he incurred Dad's wrath on the day after Oscar's encounter with Taz. You probably realized by now, Dad was a disciplinarian. His First Commandment was "Thou Shall Not Steal," and we all abided by it. So Dad became complacent when he marinated a two pound prime rib for grilling. We all salivated after it, but knew well enough to leave it alone. However, Bailey was a visitor and didn't know any better; truth to be told, I didn't think it would have made any difference. When it came to food, he was a mirror image of Auntie Sheba, minus Dad's discipline. He saw the meat and transformed himself into a homing missile. I'd say one thing for him, that puppy licked up every drop of evidence. To say Dad was upset would have been an understatement. For a while, Dad even threatened to sell Bailey to a Chinese restaurant. Thereafter, "Two Pound Dog Meat" became Beatle Bailey's nickname or "Two Pounds" for short, sometimes Dad switched it to "Dog Meat." Anyway, you got the idea. Of course, Bailey served one day in "The Cooler," and Dad swore that the JJ's would receive a bill for the prime rib that Bailey inhaled.

As for Pookie, the Burmese cat—we tolerated her presence because she was a feline, and Mom tended to look with disapproval on (PWACs) people who abused cats. Pookie also got along well with Sushi and Emily, since they were old acquaintances. Of course, she also rubbed herself against Loki's long legs to reestablish old acquaintances. Jill had groomed and shaved Pookie to resemble a miniature lion cub, with a fur ball on the end of the tail and a fan of mane around her neck. She looked good enough to strut on the catwalk.

Pookie

However, Pookie had a major phobia, she was deathly afraid of the outdoors, to say nothing of the wilderness surrounding the manor. To call her a scaredy-cat was an understatement. The furthest she would venture outside was on the deck porch. Once, Mom locked her out on the porch by accident, and it was a pitiful sight to see Pookie plastered against the window mesh screen meowing for entry. She tore halfway through the screen before Mom rushed over to let her into the house. Needless to say, that was another item on the bill for the JJ's.

Two weeks later, the JJ's returned and took their charges home. For some reason, Dad forgot to bill the JJ's for the aforementioned damages. Considering Dad's tight fisted nature, it was no minor slippage of the mind. I saw Mom's paw print in that turn of events.

That was also the last time I saw Auntie Sheba. You see, soon afterwards, the JJ's moved to California with all four of their pets—Beatle Bailey, Oscar, Pookie and Auntie Sheba.

CHAPTER 3

The People

The departure of the JJ's and their pack restored the house to some semblance of normalcy; I suppose now is as good time as any to complete the introduction of the pack.

I was the Beta of the pack. I had deferred that position to Auntie Sheba until her departure with the JJs. As I had no desire to challenge Loki, her Alpha status was secure and we liked it that way. Everybody knew his or her proper place in the pecking order. Tipping the scale at 120 pounds, I didn't have to worry about challengers for a while. I loved Loki; she took care of me and protected me when I first joined the pack as a puppy, now it was my turn to return the favor. I figured Mom and Dad liked it that way too.

Taz the Spaz was the next person in line. He's a purebred brindle Boxer. A bit small in stature for his breed, but he made up for it in speed and energy. He could outrun and out jump anyone in the pack. He liked to show off by running rings around you and teased you to try to catch him. By the way, if you were not careful, he would drown you in slobber. He was about half my size and weight, no threat to my position, and he had to go through me to challenge Loki for pack leadership.

The Three Dog Knights—Taz, Foxy Lady and Yours Truly.

Next in rank was the Princess, or the Prima Donna, depending on her mood and behavior. Dad named her Foxy Lady, with heavy drawn-out accents on the first syllables of her name so that it sounded like "Foxxy Laady." One look at her and you'd realize the genesis of her name. With long blond eye lashes and a cute pointy nose, she looked really foxy; add a big bushy plumed tail, she'd look like a Snow Fox. She came from a long line of Japanese Samurai clan called the Shiba Inu, an illustrious Japanese hunting tribe. Her cute looks and intelligence made her everyone's darling and she knew how to work the coquettish charm on people. Even though she was technically the Omega of the pack, somehow she always

THE PEOPLE

nuzzled her way onto the rim of the food bowl; except the ploy failed when it came to dealing with Loki, the Dowager Empress just gave the puppy a toothy glare, and Foxy would retreat back from the head of the food line. I believed the fact that they were of the same gender had something to do with Loki's immunity to Foxy's charm.

Personally, I adhered to the policy of ladies first. I followed Dad's example of taking the path of least resistance in dealing with dames; it avoided so much emotional turmoil and stress in the long run. There was something to be said about being happy rather than being right. The key was not to fight every battle, just win the important ones.

Oops, sorry I digressed again. That was the one bad habit I picked-up from Dad, if you let him he would talk your ears off. Anyway, to put it succinctly, there were times when you had to put your paw down to show you meant business. The trick was to exert that power of authority judiciously, to maintain order and tranquility within the pack. Loki was a good model—her mere presence deterred conflict. When necessary, she emulated Dad's throaty growl to instill discipline and order, as I described earlier in this book. It worked especially well on the kitties. No wonder Dad liked her so much; she was the teacher's pet.

Speaking of the kitties, they were the most inquisitive and weird bunch of people I had ever met. I gave up trying to understand them. They were daring darlings, I'll give them that, and they loved Loki, because she shielded them from being bullied.

Sushi

Sushi, the eldest cat was a male Siamese Ragdoll; which meant he had a gentleness that matched that of Loki. You could grab him by the tail and pull it without being scratched for your trouble. Sushi might have been the oldest member of the pack, not counting Mom and Dad of course, but he did not behave in a manner befitting his age. I never saw him lazing in the Sun; he was always on the go. A person had to be careful when you walked by a sofa or a table, a cat's paw could reach out and box you across the ear. It didn't hurt, but sure gave the victim a great scare.

Sushi enjoyed a special status within the pack; he was the only one that got to sit on the dining table during meal time (with Mom and Dad). He even snagged food from Mom and Dad's forks. It was a game for them to tease him with food. Dad's favorite trick was to hold a piece of meat in his mouth then allowed Sushi to walk up and take it away and eat it.

Believe it or not, he liked to use Dad's favorite stew pot as his private den. Good thing he (Sushi) was Mom's favorite pet, or else he might have become an entree. Sushi had a bag full of tricks to get people's attention. I already told you about his table manners, or lack thereof. His favorite move was to walk up to Mom or Dad and flop on his back with a loud thump. And if that failed to get the desired result, he would then rear up on his hind legs and spank them with his paws, sans the claws of course. Needless to say, he was the top cat of the house. However, I must say, he got along well with everybody. You heard of the story about a dog following a boy home, and got adopted into the family. Well, one day, Sushi came home from the woods with a kitten in tow. Of course the kitten became the newest member of the pack, and in honor of her benefactor, Mom named the kitten Sashimi.

Emily was a volunteer. Would you believe it? One day, she came out of nowhere and adopted Mom. Emily jumped into Mom's car without an invitation, and when Mom shooed Emily away, she somehow snuck into the house, and hid in the basement, until feeding time. After that, Mom didn't have the heart to evict her, so she became a member of the pack.

Emily

As I mentioned earlier, Emily came from a celebrated lineage; she's a Hemingway Tabby, with six toes on each of her paws. She had a sensitive, haughty personality, and generally hung out by herself. She picked her friends judiciously and apparently Mom satisfied Emily's selection criteria. Once in a while, she brought home presents for Mom and Dad, in the form of a bird or a mouse, not in a cage mind you. For some reason, the gesture was not warmly appreciated. Anyway, I wished I too had six toes on each paw; it would definitely help with traction in the mud and snow, not to mention tet-a-tet tussles.

The two cats usually got along well with each other. But, sometimes they engaged in play fighting, which always turned real, and then the fur started flying. During those times, Loki would walk up and flip the cats onto their backs with her long collie's snout. As a result, her mere appearance in the arena would put an end to the hissing contest.

We also had a parakeet named Lucy, a cockatiel named Bogee and two aquariums of fishes. Mom tried to name the fishes, but gave up after a guppy population explosion. She had gotten the birds and fishes to bring good Feng Shui into the house; birds made life musical and lively, while fishes represented prosperity. You see, Mom took Chinese traditions more seriously than Dad ever did. I personally had little interaction with those flyers and swimmers, except when they were larger and cooked that is.

The kitties tried to get at the birds, but did not succeed in catching any of them. I believed they were only teasing the birds, with no real intention of catching their prey. Of course Mom would have had a cow if the cats ever did got hold of one of her birds. On the other paw, I did spy Emily as she sat in front of the aquarium, yearning for a chance at the tasty morsels. I believe that was the reason that Dad removed all furniture near the aquariums that could be used as perches to get at the fishes.

Tom the wild turkey became an honorary member of the pack. Mom saw Tom checking out our house while it was under construction. He just walked out of the woods to greet his new neighbors, perhaps to borrow a bag of seeds? It was just before some special day that humans called "Thanksgiving." Dad immediately went hunting for his shotgun, but Mom intervened with the declaration of a new house rule—any living critter within fifty yards of the house was a pet. So that was how Tom got shot by a digital camera instead of lead pellets—lucky 'Tom.'

Lucky Tom

Oh well. But we did get to have some bites of turkey and ham later that month. By the way, I must let you know there were tracks of feral pigs in our woods, but they didn't come anywhere near the fifty yard line, so as Dad would say—"Them's fair game, fit for the pot!" Ah, there's nothing that tasted better than the crunchy skin of the Chinese roast pork, especially when it had a hunk of nice juicy meat attached to it, served with just a smidgen of ginger and garlic sauce of course. Slurp, slurp.

*   *   *

Everybody wanted to be next to Mom. As I said earlier, Foxy was a right smart girl. When she wanted to be on the sofa with Mom, a place of honor often occupied by Loki, Foxy would grab a toy and play with it in front of Loki. Inevitably, Loki couldn't resist the tease. The moment she jumped off the sofa and went after the toy, Foxy would quickly leap into the newly vacated spot then rolled over onto her back with her head in Mom's lap. At this point, Mom would only shake her head and smile at the wily ploy, and then started scratching Foxy's tummy. Before long, Foxy closed her eyes and started purring, almost catlike. Poor Loki, the wolf girl got outfoxed by the Foxy Lady.

I, on the other hand preferred a more modern and scientific approach. I would launch a chemical attack then wait for the devastating outcry, "Shadow, how could you?" Mom or Dad would immediately strike a match to burn away the nitrous stench, and cover up the aroma with the sulfurous smell, then retreat to another seat; I would then follow them to the new location and join them on the sofa. For some reason, Mom did not seem to be enamored with my attempt at bonding. She would give me that accusatory stare then fed me a bowl of yogurt after each flatulence outbreak; for some inexplicable reason, the deliciously creamy stuff always short circuited my chemical weapons system. What a drag! But, the yogurt tasted tart but good. Oh, by the way, I once tried jumping into Mom's lap a la Foxy; I knocked her and her sofa back six inches. She somehow did not appreciate my attempt at endearment as much as that of Foxy. I supposed, in that case, might did not make right.

Taz was a cry baby; he would whine and whine and whine at Mom and Dad to get what he wanted from them.

He whined for food, for walks, for playing games . . . etc. Usually, his persistence won out. What was it that they said about squeaky wheels? I'll tell you more about Taz in another chapter.

*   *   *

We had a routine around the house. Every morning, half an hour after breakfast, the whole pack would take Mom and Dad for a walk in the woods. Dad had hacked the trail with a machete then widened it with chainsaw, axe and finally, a riding lawnmower. The trail wounded through the woods for over a kilometer, so we had plenty of opportunity to explore the woods. Mom and Dad led the way, with the pack (mostly dogs) running around them. Often Sushi would join us on the march and, believe it or not, he even squatted in the woods to "potty" with us. *What a cat!*

Loki, being part wolf, usually walked in front as the scout. One time she flushed a deer out of the bushes, creating an instant excitement among the pack. Of course, no one expected the encounter and the deer made a clean get away. Not that we could have done anything anyway. You should have been there to see Loki's face. She grinned from ear to ear and loped from bush to bush like a young wolf cub. Ever since then, Loki forgot her arthritic aches and looked forward to the daily walks. Mom often seeded the woods with leftover potato chips, pop corns or cheese noodles. So it became a scavenger hunt every time we went into the woods;

even though the chips were supposed to be for wild critters, but as they say—*finder's keepers and losers weepers*. However, you should know that I did not participate in the junk food smorgasbord; I preferred being lean and mean over fat and sassy.

*   *   *

In the afternoons, weather permitting, Mom and Dad usually played fetch with us. They threw stuffed toys from the porch down the hill behind the house then we had to run down the porch stairs to fetch them back. Well, after running a few laps between the porch, the stairs and the hill, the fun part quickly wore thin. That was when I took the matter, "the toy" I meant, into my own jaws. After one final round of panting run down the hill then back, instead of returning the toy to Mom and Dad, I brought it into the house and hid it, putting an end to the game for that day.

Dad, being a Chinese, was a creature of habit, therefore a trainable subject. We conditioned him into taking us for walks during evenings. He liked to work (play games) on his computer after dinner, and we would gather around him. I would lay my chin on his thigh, and Foxy would nozzle his calf, while Taz whined and whined incessantly, all under the supervision of Loki who waited patiently by the cane stand with Sheba at her side. We jointly focused our brains on walking in the woods, inevitably the telepathic linkage succeed in penetrating Dad's skull as he rose to his feet; that was the signal for us to yelp and cheer, and run circles around him to praise him for listening to us. *That's what psychologists call positive reinforcement.* In time, he learned to take us for walks after supper, without us telling him to do so. And that was how you got humans to respond to your desires.

Now, you should know that we had over a dozen thick blankets, pet beds and cushions strategically positioned throughout the house. They were fine for short rests and naps during the day; however, at bedtime, everybody wanted to snuggle with Mom and Dad. Wouldn't you? At night, Taz was always the first one in bed. Sometimes, the cats would be there with him, snuggled into a fur ball (the cats I meant). We big boys and girls didn't get in bed until Mom and Dad were settled in there, otherwise Dad would shoo us off (the bed), so that they could climb in. Anyway, it was a full house when everybody finally got comfortable—Mom, Dad, five dogs and three cats. It was all nice and cozy in the winter, but the bed got down right hot and musty in the dog days of the summer months with all ten of us, even if it was a king sized job. Dad complained that it felt like sleeping in a strait jacket under a ton of bones. Personally, I didn't know what he was talking about. The only bony one in the pack was Taz the Spaz, and we all agreed that Auntie Sheba was downright Rubenesque.

And, it became a major "packfield in motion" when Mom or Dad had to make nature calls at night. Whoever slept near Mom or Dad had to jump off to allow them to go do their business. Of course, when they returned from their constitution, everyone unpacked again and waited around until Mom and Dad got comfortably settled back between the sheets.

*   *   *

Mom and Dad had nicknames for most of us. Loki was also known as Wolfie Girl because of her lycanthrope heritage; often, for no reason, she would howl like her ancestors, especially if a shiny full moon hung in the sky outside of the window. Personally, I thought she missed her calling as a model. With her long thin legs, regal carriage and fine shiny coat, she would have been a real knockout on any cat walk.

Auntie Sheba answered to Miss Piggy for obvious reasons. Her sleek blue-black hair made her look like a pudgy Nubian Princess. She had a docile and ultra friendly personality, I never saw her participate in a dog fight, a rare occurrence for a dog. Her jovial personality might have been partially responsible for her excess weight; she never engaged in any physical competition, such as play fights, tug-of-war . . . etc.

I was known as Tall Dark and Handsome, yuck, yuck, snort, snort. I'll tell you more about me in a separate chapter devoted entirely to myself.

Taz the Spaz's legal name was Tasmanian Tiger, inspired by the brindle tiger stripes on his body. "The Spaz" was an add-on to his name given by Mom for his clumsy, spastic behavior; however, Dad liked to call him Dracu Dog, because

Taz often slept on his back, and in that position his loose jowl skins flapped back so that his face looked like a blood sucking bat with widespread wings and a full set of fangs.

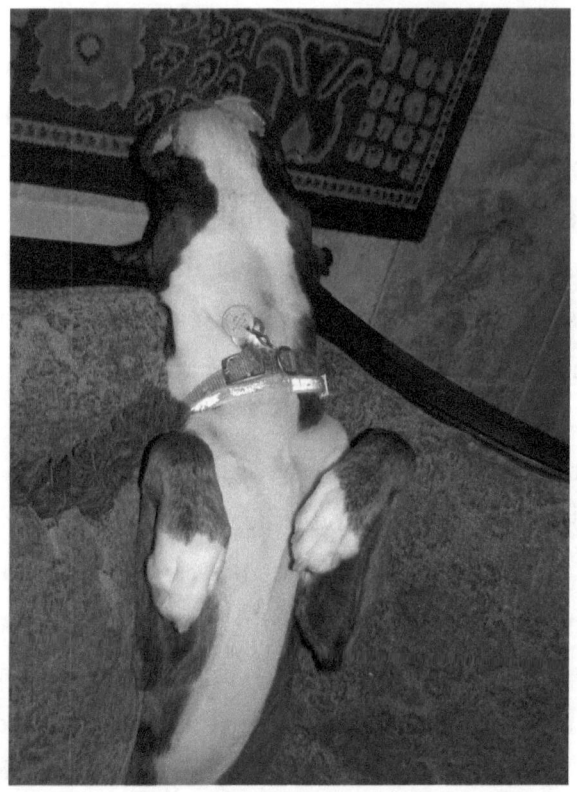

Taz (AKA: Dracu Dog)

Coincidentally, Dad liked to tease him by grabbing hold of those loose jaw flaps/bat wings and shake them sideways. In retaliation, Taz shook his head quickly, showering Dad with saliva, followed by a wave of fierce and physical tongue lashing.

THE PEOPLE

Believe it or not, Foxy had the unlikely nickname of "Killer." She held the record for most kills—ten and a half opossums plus one rat and a mole. She shared half the credit of one opossum kill with Taz. In this case, her breeding held true, she definitely was a good hunter.

As a scion of the famous Hemingway, Emily naturally got the nickname of Margaux (Hemingway) in honor of her genetic six toed heritage. She was a loner, and would have nothing to do with anybody except Loki and Sushi, plus Mom and Dad, of course. Good thing, she did not ambush us like Sushi did, otherwise her extra claws might have done serious damages.

Sushi was unique in that he never acquired a nickname; but he's everybody's friend, especially us dogs. Sushi often used the sofa as his massage table. He would jump on the sofa and groom us as we rested our chins on the arm rest of the sofa. I loved the sensation of the sandpaper like tongue on my face. It felt so good that I sometimes fell asleep under his grooming ministration.

And the junior of the pack, Sashimi received the nickname of "Mao Mi" by way of Grandpa Ye Ye. Mao Mi literally meant "little kitty" in Chinese. She was a playful kitten, which appealed to Grandpa's sense of propriety. What grandfather would not dote on the youngest member of the clan?

As a pack, we tended to prefer Mom over Dad because Dad was the enforcer while Mom was Mom, and we could always wheedle her into our way of doing things. However, I must say Loki favored Dad, probably because Dad was a male. Every time Mom and Dad had a sparring contest Loki would jump in between them and bark at Mom to protect Dad from her. Of course, we all knew they were only play fighting, but Loki couldn't help stopping any conflicts. A most unusual trait for a wolf, but I supposed it might have been the due to her gentle Collie genes, or the desire for pack tranquility.

When Dad left town on business trips, Loki always slept on his pillow. Of course, when he got home, he had to change the pillow case because Loki always left a thick layer of wolf fur on his pillow as a welcome home present. You can't believe how much fur she she'd shed! Dad said that was due to Loki's wolf ancestry. However, Dad never got upset at Loki for sleeping on his pillow. He just changed the pillow case and dropped the subject. Did I mention that she was his favorite number one girl?

CHAPTER 4

"Rip"

Grand Pa "Rip" (file photo)

Grandpa Leo, Mom's Dad, had been a Navy test pilot and claimed to have been a plank holder of that infamous Tail Hook Association. In Naval phraseology, a "Plank Holder" was an original founder of an organization or tradition. At almost six feet with a full red beard, he cut a dashing figure. His name was Leonard, but he preferred to go by "Rip," his Naval aviator *call sign*; it was short for "Rip Roaring Rohrer."

For an octogenarian, his range and pace of activities made people half his age feel ancient and tired. After multiple airplane crashes, emergency aircraft landings and two bicycled run-ins (with trucks), he finally slowed down a bit, but nothing could diminish his sense of humor and the penchant for mischief. He lived life to the fullest extent possible, to the awe and chagrin of his many acquaintances. Dad referred to it as Rip's "Lust for Life."

He lived not far away from us with his French Poodle, Nicky; they were regulars around the Stump Tish—A German term which meant "Reserved Table" for special regular customers to the Pets Only. Dad brought the tradition back from Germany, and it became an immediate hit with the steady clientele from the neighborhood. I liked it too because I knew all the patrons at that table and they acknowledged my *enforcer* position at the Inn, which translated to *food*.

One warm summer day, Grandpa Rip arrived without advance notice. Instead of Nicky, he brought a new friend, an African Gray parrot. He thrusted the birdcage into Dad's hands and commanded in a no uncertain tone, "This bird is supposed to be able to talk. Teach her some

"Rip"

Chinese!" And that was how Gracie became a member of the pack. Of course, Rip got himself a resident companion for entry into Pets Only. I'd say it was a very slick piece of maneuvering on the part of Rip. He got the benefit of owning the pet bird without having to feed her or clean the cage, not to mention free Chinese language lessons for Gracie, plus a permanent passport for entry into Pets Only. I'd say Rip pulled off a fast one on Dad. What do you think?

After handing over the bird, Rip inquired on the whereabouts of his daughter, and learned that Mom had gone fishing at the pond with Kimberly. With a twinkle in his eyes, Rip marched into the kitchen and fished out a Sea Bass from the freezer. He nuked the fish on low power for a minute to thaw it slightly then placed it inside a plastic bag before heading out toward the pond. Out of curiosity, I trailed behind to check out his newest caper.

Kimberly was a precocious five year old neighbor that liked to hang out with us. Dad called her his "favorite number one neighbor." She would retort with "And you are my favorite number one Chinese neighbor;" the fact that he was the only Chinese neighbor within twenty miles notwithstanding. She had the run of the grounds, and everyone accepted her as a member of the pack. However, Taz initially got into his spastic moods and tried to alpha her. Poor puppy, he soon came to realize the errors of his ways.

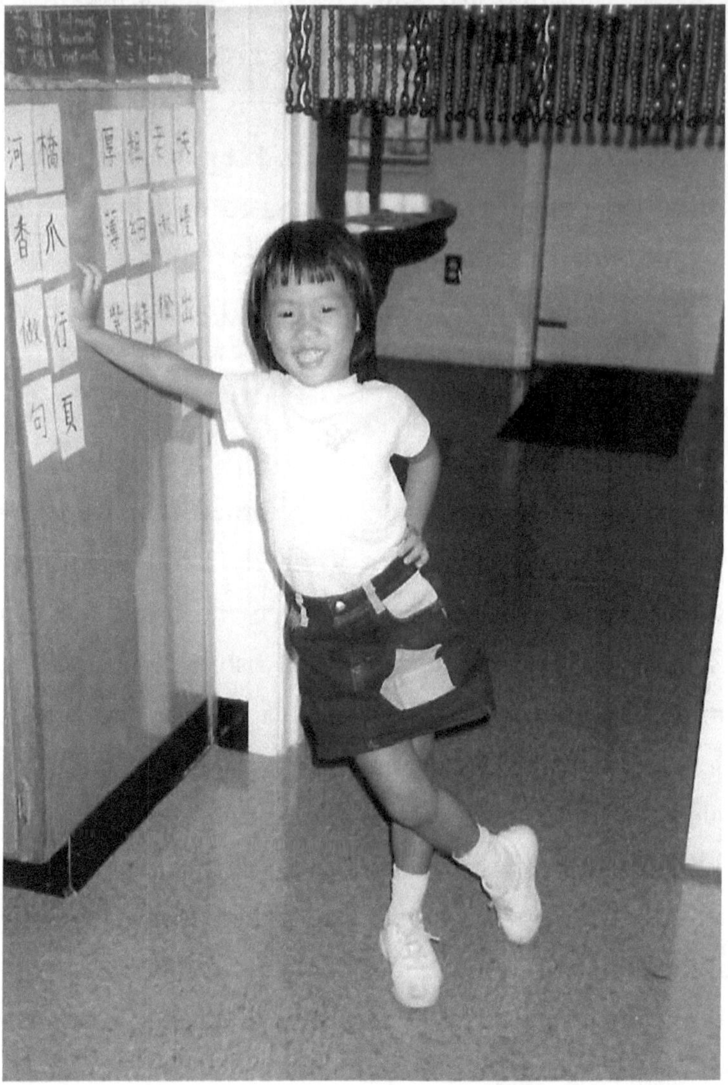

Kimberly the Taz tamer

You see, Taz nipped at her and swiped food out of her hands to intimidate her. Naturally, Kimberly ran away crying after the encounter. Mom saw what happened and calmly

"Rip"

soothed Kimberly then reminded her of the pack psychology lessons Dad had preached. You could visibly see her spirits return and her eyes brightened with mischief; she rolled up a tube of newspaper then marched toward her tormentor. In a stern voice, she ordered Taz, "Stay!" then proceeded to administer a few good whacks across the rump (Taz's) with her weapon. Obviously cowered by Kimberly's domineering bearing, Taz quickly rolled onto his back and whimpered in submission. That measure kept Taz in his place for a while, before he built up enough courage to try it again.

After the second bullying attempt from Taz, Kimberly decided that the best defense was a good offense—another of Dad's adage. She started by intentionally shoving Taz out of his comfortable seat on his favorite sofa, so that she could sit in his spot, even though there were plenty of other seats available nearby. Then, she'd command "Stay!" to Taz, and while the dog stood still, she tied a tube sock around his stubby snout. His pitiful whines brought chuffing laughter and ridicule until Mom came around to rescue him.

Finally, Kimberly placed a large pink paper flower around Taz's neck then ordered "Heel!" Poor Taz had to "heel" by her side, walked at her pace and sat down by her side when she stopped. It was quite a sight to see Taz trailing docilely beside a little girl half his size, with a large pink paper flower encircling his neck. After that, Taz gave up any further attempt to alpha Kimberly and they became the best of friends.

But I digress. As I was saying, Rip snuck up to the pond and slipped into the water under the dock. I trotted up to

Mom and Kimberly then lied down to take in some rays, and watch the plot unfold.

Before you could say "lickety spit," the girls were jumping for joy on the dock. They had hooked a catch. Suddenly, a much waterlogged Rip appeared at their sides to help land the fish. For some reason, the fish hung limp on the line, but Kimberly was too excited to notice that it had already been gutted and cleaned; at the same time no one mentioned the miracle of catching a salt water Sea Bass in a fresh water pond. I did spy Mom smile wryly, rolled her eyes then shook her head at her own impish father as he happily helped Kimberly unhook her catch.

Later, Dad served fish as "The Chinese supplise," and yummy yummy; Pan Fried Sea Bass with sweet and spicy sauce was one of my favorite dishes. The crispy crunchy tail and fins were just too tasty to describe.

That evening, after dinner, Foxy Lady proudly trotted into the living room and presented a large bunny to Mom. I didn't mean a stuffed toy; I meant a real big white rabbit. We all recognized it to be "Big Foot," the house pet of Jabba the Hutt, our next door neighbor. By the way he hung in Foxy's muzzle, you knew Big Foot had hopped for the last time. Surprisingly, there was neither blood nor gashes on his skin. Apparently, Foxy had given the rabbit a heart attack.

Mom dropped her tea cup and screamed hysterically, "Daddy! Daddy! Take that thing away. Daddy!"

Dad sighed aloud then reluctantly started to rise from his seat to do her bidding, but unexpectedly, Rip nonchalantly laid down his newspaper and got to his feet. He reached over to pat Dad on the shoulder and pushed him back onto his chair. Rip winked his eyes at Dad as he commanded, "Sit! I distinctly heard her said Daddy, are you her Daddy? I'll take care of it." Dad's eyes widened slightly in surprise as he perceived the advent of another one of Rip's antics; he smiled conspiratorially and nodded in acquiescence.

Mom eyed Rip's retreating backside then turned to look accusingly at Dad, "Well, what are you going to do? *Your* daughter killed Big Foot, how are you going to explain it to Jabba?"

"Me? How come she is always *your* good girl when she behaves then transforms into *my* daughter when she messes up?" As if to punctuate the point, Foxy leaped upon the sofa, rolled onto her back with her head in Mom's lap then stuck out her tongue at Dad as she panted for a belly rub.

"Well, you figure it out and take care of it," Mom said while she reflexively responded to Foxy's demand and started to scratch her tummy, who crooned contentedly and closed her eyes luxuriating under Mom's gentle fingers.

Ten minutes later, Rip walked into the room panting lightly, but grinning from ear to ear. At Mom's questioning look, he dropped the smile and gave her a boy scout's two finger salute, and announced "Mission accomplished, madam." Mom and Dad glanced at each other but did not say a word. At long last, Rip couldn't resist the silent treatment, "Alright, alright would you two relax? Big Foot was already dead this afternoon. On my way here, I came across Jabba; the man had been crestfallen that his pet rabbit had died of old age. Apparently, he had buried Big Foot in the woods, the only problem was that he was too lazy to dig a proper deep hole, as Foxy demonstrated when she dug up Big Foot and brought him home."

"And what did you do with Big Foot, just now?" asked Mom.

"Oh, nothing much, I just put him back where he belonged," he responded innocently, then picked up the pen and resumed his work on the crossword section of the funny papers. Mom gave him a stern look of exasperation but refused to be goaded into another bout of fruitless verbal jousting.

"Rip"

*　　　　*　　　　*

The next day, Jabba limped all excited into Pets Only with his pet, Bubba, in tow. You see, Jabba was a biker who had had an unfortunate close encounter of the personal kind with an oak tree, and his left knee had suffered from the incident, ergo the limp. As for his companion, Bubba was a bully and we didn't get along well, but that was another story for another time.

As I was saying, Jabba came into the restaurant with an ashy look, as though he'd seen a ghost. Now, believe it or not, Jabba did not normally drink alcoholic beverages. So it was a surprise to us all when he sat down and ordered a beer. He took a long pull of the drink then exhaled and belched loudly, "Aaah, I needed that," a slight pause "we have ghosts in these here woods." He glanced around the bar as if looking for a specter to appear; "there are ghosts in these woods I tell ya," he repeated, waited in vain for a follow-up rejoinder then added, "You know my pet rabbit, Big Foot? He died yesterday. I took him into the woods and buried him. And this morning, he was back in his cage. Aside from a few smudges of dirt on his white fur, he looked just like when he was still alive."

"Perhaps, you were mistaken; you might have buried him alive, and he dug himself out of the grave, maybe?" Dad said, as he exchanged a knowing glance with Mom. "Where is Big Foot now? Is he dead? Or still alive and kicking?"

"Still in his cage, and I ain't going near it."

"You mean like he turned zombie, right?" Mom jumped into the fray. Mom loved vampire and horror movies, so she started warming up to the subject.

Jabba merely shuddered and nodded his head.

"Well, you'd better go check and see if he's still alive, or turned zombie." Mom goaded him. "Either way, you have to go home, unless you intend to abandon the house to a dead or a zombie rabbit."

Jabba mulled over Mom's words then searched in vain for assistance. No one volunteered to face the bunny zombie. Reluctantly, Jabba crushed his empty beer can then lumbered out of the Inn with Bubba trailing behind.

That evening, at Rip's most insistent suggestion, Dad served "Rabbit Stew" as the 'Chinese supplise' item at Pets Only. For some inexplicable reason, Jabba decided not to partake in the special of the day.

By the way, just in case you were interested, it (the rabbit) tasted liked a stringy old hen; definitely not one of my personal favorite menu item.

For the next few days, Gracie added a new tune to her repertoire; as the dirge from 'Adams Family' became the theme song at Pets only. I wondered if Rip had a hand in that new musical number.

"Rɪᴘ"

CHAPTER 5

Jabba the Hutt

Jabba, the aforementioned master of the zombie Big Foot, had the reputation as a walking disaster area. Trouble followed him everywhere he went. Loquacious and determined, he liked to dispense advice on all subject matters, while firmly convinced that everyone should agree with his point of view. Needless to say, he did not have many friends. We tolerated him because it was the neighborly thing to do. He was tall, with full facial and body fur except for the bald patch on the crown of his head, and weighed a rotund 350 pounds. Supposedly, the JJs had given him the moniker because he reminded them of a slovenly fat slug in some popular science fiction classic. Dad agreed that the man's physical and personal traits did resemble the space gangster in that epic movie. I believe Jabba was short for "Jabba the Hutt." I wasn't a sci-fi fan, so I had no idea what Dad was talking about. Of course Jabba was not his original name, but I had no idea what was the man's original name.

Personally, in view of his height, weight, furry pelt, lumbering gait and most significantly the odorous stench, I thought Sasquatch, or "Squatch," might have been a more suitable moniker. But, what do I know, I am only a dog and nobody ever asked for my opinion.

Jabba had two dogs, but he never took them for walks. As a result, the area around his home became a fecal minefield that everyone avoided. Dad called it a toxic waste dump, filled with biological hazards. On a warm day, you could smell the stench from ten miles away. As for Jabba, your nose (human and animals alike) would detect his presence long before you heard his lumbering footsteps.

Jabba lived with two dogs, the elder of the two was the aforementioned Bubba, a black Rottie mix. The other was Jappy, a yappy female Pincher mix. Bubba was a bully, and she used to harass me when I was a puppy, when Loki or Dad weren't around that is. Dad had trained Bubba, but that was before I joined the pack; so she knew the proper etiquette when she accompanied Jabba to Pets Only.

Jappy and I were puppy buddies, because Bubba had abused her too—you know the Chinese adage, "the enemy of my enemy is my friend." So Jappy and I joined forces and ganged up against Bubba, which ended the bullying for good (as far as we were concern). As they say, united we stand. The fact that I eventually outweighed Bubba by 40 pounds, and knew all of her fighting techniques helped dampen her aggressiveness.

Bubba resumed his bullying habits when Taz joined the pack. But Dad was an effective deterrent against Bubba's bullying, and Dad did not let Taz run loose until he had been well schooled in the pack etiquette. By the time Bubba finally got a chance to lay a paw on the Boxer, they were almost of equal size, except Bubba weighted twenty pounds more than Taz. However, the bully lacked the speed and agility to inflict any serious damage to the fastest paw in the pack. So, once again Bubba became a frustrated, unhappy camper. As with all dogs, Bubba liked to romp free in the woods. The problem was, Jabba never took her for walks, thus Bubba often went AWOL. Thus, trouble arose when she had to be brought home by the County Animal Control Officers, who gave Jabba a lecture regarding the responsibilities of a dog owner. Needless to say, Bubba went into lockdown, which only exacerbated the situation.

Jabba, being a typical hillbilly, had two loves—bikes and dogs. His chopped black and gold Harley-Davidson Fat Boy with silvery chrome pipes was nothing to slouch at. When not in use, he kept it covered under the carport. It was the only things that Jabba liked to work on and keep clean.

One day, after Bubba was brought home by way of the County Animal Control, Jabba decided to teach the dog a lesson by leashing her on a metal post of the carport with a long chain, while he went out with a friend. Well, Taz happened to trot by Jabba's place, and Bubba welcomed Taz with angry barks while straining against the leash chain. Noting Bubba's limited range of mobility, Taz's adventuresome spirit came to the fore. He ran up to Bubba then hopped in place a few times like a kangaroo, stimulating and agitating Bubba to the point of frothing at the mouth. Taz then trotted from one side of the carport to the other, just out of the other dog's reach; while the very excited Bubba followed on the end of the chain. To make a long story short, in the process of trying to get at Taz, Bubba repeatedly dragged the long chain over the Hog, wrapped the chain around the bike, tipped it on its side then dragged it over the gravel. The maneuver snapped off the side view mirrors, cracked the windshield and last but not least, tore up the saddle bag and broke off a muffler pipe.

I leave you to imagine Bubba's predicament when Jabba got home; it wasn't a pretty sight. I didn't know what punishment Bubba received, but we didn't see her for one whole week. Oh well, I might not have liked Bubba, but I still felt sorry for her. As for Taz, he'd better keep his running paws ready and have an eye peeled for Bubba. I wondered if Jabba ever found out the real culprit of the damages to his bike.

The day after the battle of the carport, Jabba called his friend JD, a mechanic, to assess the damages to the bike. JD arrived with a German Sheppard named Kaiser in the flatbed of his F-150 pick-up. JD whistled and shook his head as he walked around the carport to survey the damages before pronouncing his findings, "The damages were mostly superficial and cosmetic, except for the mirrors, wind shield and the muffler. With me doing the work, it would cost you about a thousand dollars for parts and labor."

Jabba breathed heavily and grunted, "Alright, let's go to Pets Only to go over the repairs needed for the bike. Besides, I want to show you our local landmark."

Loki and Gracie greeted them at the entrance with a synchronized, "Woof, woof; welcome." JD blinked in surprise and waved his hand in greeting to the maitre de, who lifted her right paw in return. JD next reached over to pet Gracie, but Dad interceded, "Careful, unless you wish to lose your finger. By the way, where is your pet?" At JD's questioning look, Dad added, "No pets, no service. Sorry, that's the house rule."

Jabba grinned at the surprised look of his wide eyed companion, "JD, no pets means no service. You gotta bring Kaiser in with us. The food is great. The alternative is twenty minutes drive away, and not as good tasting." Doubtfully, JD brought Kaiser into Pets Only. The Sheppard seemed a little skittish, so Loki and I exchanged sniffs with him to calm him then seated the trio in a secluded stall at the far end of the bar, which had a grassy open area for pets.

Jabba obviously wanted to show off his familiarity of the establishment; he nonchalantly slapped the bar with his palm and proudly placed his order, "One order of pot stickers, two shawarmas and two cokes," then followed Loki to their table. He noticed that JD had tethered Kaiser to the hitching post on the lawn. Being an animal lover, Jabba believed that all animals would reciprocate his amicable personality; he decided to get better acquainted with the dog.

JD warned, "Don't do that, he doesn't know you yet. He's skittish of strangers." Jabba smiled confidently and said, "Nah, that there dog won't bite me." He confidently reached his hand over to pet Kaiser then immediately withdrew the bloodied limb and yelled, "Ouch, he bit me!" Well, he did not receive any sympathy from anybody, except for Gracie, who serenaded him with the opening bar from MASH.

Say what you will, Jabba loved animals. The other day, Emily climbed a tall pine tree, and got stuck up there. I didn't know how long had she been up there before anyone realized her predicament. Eventually, her meowing attracted Dad's attention, but no amount of calling and anchovies could get Emily to climb down on her own. In desperation, Dad went and got some help in the form of Jabba. After a half hour of fruitless coaxing, Jabba suggested they cut down a neighboring tree, so that it would fall and lean against the tree that Emily was on to create a ramp for her to climb down to the ground. Dad pondered the idea then went to the garage to get his chainsaw.

The two good Samaritans used the chainsaw to start a notch in the selected tree. The sloping ground made cutting difficult and dangerous; the curvy tree trunk and the blustery wind did not make the job any easier. After the notch had been cut, they were ready to make the final slice. Dad looked at the tall swaying pine, and commented "You see the way this tree sways in the wind? It may not fall in the right direction." Jabba lifted his head to look at tree then sneered arrogantly, "I'll make that tree fall any way I want. You just finish the cut and I'll push it in the right direction." So saying, he started pushing the tree as Dad started up the chainsaw. Next thing you knew, the tree snapped and fell on top of Jabba, pushing his chest against the freshly cut stump, in the process, he cracked two ribs. Meanwhile, Dad shut down the chainsaw and laid it down safely aside before going to check on Jabba. During the commotion, Emily climbed on a long tree branch, leaped over to another tree and scampered down to the ground. I guess she didn't really need any help after all. Woof, woof.

As Jabba had been hurt while rendering assistance to Dad, it became a moral obligation for Dad to help Jabba obtain medical treatment. Poor Dad, he had to hold his breath while helping Jabba walk out of the woods, and into the Inn. While Dad called for an ambulance, Gracie tilted her head and greeted them at the bar with her newly acquired quip, "Need a drink?" Dad thought it was pretty funny and rewarded Gracie with a handful of sunflower seeds. Jabba gave Gracie an ugly stare, then couldn't help but join in with a chuckle, which promptly turned into a grimace. I guessed the laughter must have accidentally pulled some nerve or muscle in his chest, causing a pain spasm. At least Jabba had a sense of humor.

For a while, Jabba's latest bout with disaster remained a favorite subject of discussion at the Stump Tish, until something more interesting happened along. As for me, I stayed away from Jabba as much as possible for aromatic and hygienic reasons, and providence. One should always avoid potential arenas of calamity. Life contained sufficient hazards as it was; therefore, I saw no reason to court more disaster by being physically close to Jabba.

CHAPTER 6

Faraj and Ray Ray

Ray Ray, one of Dad's best friends in the neighborhood, lived only a quarter mile away from us. He had so many pets that I couldn't keep track of all their names. They included a donkey named Nell, a herd of goats, a flock of sheep, and a yellow Golden Retriever named "Goldie," of course. They were nice people, especially Nell; but, when she brayed, it sounded like she was raising the dead, and you could hear her from a quarter mile away. I knew this, because I heard her braying all the time. The first day Ray Ray brought Nell home, Mom heard Nell's bray and thought it had came from a giant bull frog; she said "That's got to be the mother of all bull frogs!" Dad laughed and had to gently disillusion her, "No, sweetheart, that's just Ray Ray's new jackass." You should realize that we had lots of bullfrogs near our creek and fish pond, and I must say they (Nell and the bullfrogs) did sound very much alike, especially during evenings of the mating season.

"Faraj" was the pet sheep that Ray Ray kept on hand for entry into Pets Only. Ray Ray was an Iraqi Shiite, and Arabs generally preferred cats over dogs as pets; but cats didn't take to leashes very well. Of course, some people could leash-train cats, but that's few and far in between. They were just too darn

fickle and independent; whereas a sheep was more pliant as long as you kept them happy with food. That was how Faraj became Ray Ray's companion to Pets Only.

Since Dad and Ray Ray were good buddies, he had the run of the house and the Inn. I liked Ray Ray, because he treated me like a friend and cooked a mean fish. Regularly, he would bring a sea bass to Pets Only, and grilled it over the BBQ pit a la Iraqi style called Masgouf. I can't cook, but I knew how a good fish should taste. If you haven't tried Masgouf, you should give it a bite. Trust me, just like potato chips, you can't take only one.

The other day, Ray Ray arrived toting a shopping bag which contained a fresh sea bass, with a well behaved Faraj in tow. He exchanged ritual hugs and cheek greetings with everyone, and gave me a quick friendly pat and rub of my head. I sniffed Faraj face to welcome her to Pets Only.

Ray Ray headed straight for the BBQ grill to work on the fish, which had already been split open from the spine and cleaned of its innards. He rubbed the fish with extra virgin olive oil, garlic and sea salt. After rubbing olive oil on six long skewers, Ray Ray used them to pierce the fish with the head and skin intact. Standing the skewers like a tripod, he leaned the fish over the BBQ grill at a forty-five degree angle. Before you knew it, the pungent aroma of grilled garlic started wafting through the restaurant. Another twenty minutes, and the fish skin started turning crispy. Ray Ray took the fish off the grill, squeezed and rubbed half a lemon, salt and pepper on the fleshy side of the fish. He then laid the fish back on the grill with the flesh side down. While the fish cooked on the grill, Ray Ray spread a thick layer of newspaper on the Stump Tish. Five minutes later, he brought the fish over and laid it on the newspaper, and invited everyone to dig in. Hassan laid out a steaming tray of basmati rice, chopped onion and tomatoes, Arabian flat bread, hummus, cucumber dips and olives to accompany the fish. Everyone reached in with their hands and grabbed chunks of the fish. For those people that did not like fish, Hassan set out a plate of Shawarma so that they too could join us in the festivities. No problem, it meant more fish for the rest of us. Of course we four legged folk had to wait patiently for our share. I just loved the crispy burnt texture of the fish skin.

After they cleared the table, Ray Ray challenged Dad to a ritual game of backgammon. Midway through the game, Faraj had finished munching his pile of hay and became bored with the environment. He obviously wanted to head for home. He repeatedly nudged and bumped Ray Ray with his head, to no avail. Annoyed with the kibitzing sheep, Ray Ray slapped Faraj on the head after several rounds of nudging from the sheep. With each slap of the head, Faraj would back away then return after the stinging sensation had worn off.

As expected, Ray Ray won the game (he was the local champion, while Dad was still a novice at the game). Ray Ray checked the time then gathered up the tether to lead Faraj toward home. Being a devout Shiite, Ray Ray ritually prayed to the southeast toward Mecca five times a day. Since it was time for his afternoon prayer, Ray Ray led the goat up to the hill top near the restaurant and turned to face southeast. He unrolled the prayer rug and knelt down to start his religious ritual. Just as his head touched the ground, he heard running hoof beats coming up behind him, followed by a sharp pain on his backside. Next thing he knew, he was somersaulting down the hill, and did not stop tumbling until he had landed in a blackberry patch. It was a stunningly stinging experience, to say the least. Looking back up the hill, he saw Faraj bobbing his horned head and grinning down at him. Needless to say, Ray Ray's encounter with Faraj immediately replaced Jabba's latest misadventure atop the gossip menu at Pets Only.

However, I must mention that in spite of Faraj's misdeed, Ray Ray did not consign him to the stew pot, for Faraj was a pet, thus not a viable source of protein. I do like a man with a proper sense of rectitude; however, for some reason thereafter, Goldie became Ray Ray's regular companion to Pets Only.

By the way, Ray Ray went somersaulting down the same hill and in the same aerodynamic style that Taz had sent Oscar on his flying lesson. Personally, I thought they both could use some trapeze lessons, their forms as they tumbled through the air were just not aesthetically correct.

For a while, Gracie would trill the Islamic call to prayer every time she saw Ray Ray enter the inn. I believed Hassan had something to do with the creation of that musical rendition.

CHAPTER 7

Food Glorious Food

If you did not realize it by now, allow me to educate you. Chinese considered food as the most important subject in a person's existence. Their logic went like this—Man's duty to himself and his ancestors was to propagate and continue the existence of the race. In order to continue the race, he/she must have nutrients, namely food. All of this was summed up by a famous Chinese sage, Confucius, who said—"Food and Sex" were the most basic of our natural needs; ergo, the purpose of this chapter.

As the alpha of the pack, Loki had the undisputed first bite at food. But, Mom and Dad always made sure the rest of us got ours. The problem was that once in a while, at meal time, Loki would gather up all the food bowls, and pile them between her front paws before eating from all of them. Of course, in the process of collecting the bowls, she scattered half the food all over the floor. What followed was a free for all, everyone hurried to scarf up the spilt food then went whining collectively to Mom and Dad for justice. They would always grumble at Loki then take the food bowls away from her to give them back to us, and stood by to make sure Loki did not repeat her antics, but no further punishment beyond that. Loki would behave for a month or so then returned to the same antics. It was her way of reinforcing her alpha position; which sort of explained the reason that Mom and Dad allowed her to have her way. Oh well, as they say you can't fight city hall, so deal with it. Personally, I believed it must have been that time of the month that females regularly had to go through. I noticed that Foxy was extra snappy around that same time of the month.

We all loved food, but in different ways. Believe it or not, I am a gourmand. I knew the difference between slop and dining. I, for one, was very particular about my diet. I refused to eat starchy food, such as pasta, rice or bread—too much carbs was not good for your health, so I had been told by Mom. I would take cheese, but only the gourmet cheese, none of that el cheapo single-wrap stuff you get by the pound in supermarkets. Occasionally I would eat bacon, but bacon grease was the preferred licking material. As you must have realized by now, my favorite foodstuffs were meat and dairy products. Gourmet cheese and cream, any type of cream, were on the top of my yummy list. Once, Mom gave me a slice of creamy peanut butter on toast. I licked-up all the peanut butter then returned the toast to her and asked for a refill (of the peanut butter). If you didn't believe me, just ask her. To say she was surprised would have been a major understatement. Dad got a good chuckle out of that incident and never got tired of reiterating it to his friends. Oh, I almost forgot to mention, I also loved seafood: fresh fish, shrimp, lobsters, or scallops served with creamy cheese sauce with loads of garlic . . . ahhhhh, those were food I would willingly beg for.

Now, liking food was a mental desire, while acquiring it was an art. I never barked, whined or begged for food. My tactics involved patience and letting my one hundred and twenty pound presence speak for me. Of course, raining saliva out of the sides of my jaw increased the sympathy factor, providing additional emphasis to the intended point. When that too failed, the next move entailed resting my chin on the table, for I stood tall enough to do so. A puddle of drool on the table delivered a clear message. The technique of final resort involved chuffing then shaking my head violently, the intended purpose being to fling liquid droplets in the direction of food platters; some of the saliva would, hopefully, land strategically into those plates of food. Usually, I didn't need to deploy that last drastic head shaking routine. Like I always said, Mom and Dad were easily trainable subjects. They knew the proper response to my subtle hints and that was how one went about staking claim on the yum-yums; slurp, slurp.

Taz was an omnivore, he did not merely eat, he literally inhaled food into his belly. Mom said that was typical of Boxers, and such dining habit might cause bloat in Taz's stomach, which could turn deadly. So, Taz got served his meal with a large piece of rock in his food bowl. It forced Taz to slow down and ate around the obstacle, ergo no bloat; poor puppy.

Taz had his own repertoire of food acquisition techniques. He liked to rest his chin on top of Dad's thigh, drooling all over his pants legs, accompanied by occasional keening. At times, Taz would unwittingly display a unique routine which always produced positive results. I said unwittingly because if he had truly mastered the technique, he would have used it all the time, which he did not. Anyway, as I was saying, he would salivate at the sight of food then breathed air into the hanging drool, thus creating beautiful shiny bubbles. Mom and Dad loved to watch as the bubbles increased in size; some of them got as large as Taz's head, and even reflected sunlight in rainbow colors. They would dangle food in front of Taz then waited to see the drool bubble show. Personally, I'd classify that under pet abuse or torture. But, I didn't think it left any psychological scars. Besides, Taz always got rewarded with the treat at the end of the show.

By the way, I needed to warn you about a commercial product called "Ole Yummy." Once, in a moment of ACSF (acquired Chinese sense of frugality), Mom bought a large bag of the Ole Yummy dry food. It flunked the quality control test when Auntie Sheba spat them out of her mouth. The sight was downright comical to see chunks of the stuff flying out of her mouth, bouncing down the stairwell, then disappeared into the basement. I mean, when even the world's number one chow machine refused to eat, that was a major no-go. I saw Loki kept nosing through her bowl, seeking edible morsels, to no avail, leaving scattered bits of the "Ole Yummy" kibbles all around her food bowl. As for me, I just waited for handouts from Mom and Dad at their meal time. Of course my human friends at the Inn were always good for some emergency rations.

However, the problem remained; what to do with the raunchy fare? Tossing it was out of the question, it went against the miserly Chinese grain to throw good food away, even crummy tasteless slop. Anyway, Grandpa Ye-Ye boiled a large pot of pork bones and added the greasy soup over bowls of Ole Yummy. It still took almost a week, and literal near starvation, before we finally saw the last of Ole Yummy in our daily menu. I was sure the accusatory looks everyone directed at Mom kept her from ever making the same mistake again.

You must have realized by now that we nibbled often; whenever Mom and Dad ate, we always got a few bites of their food. At the least, we got to lick their plates. Additionally, Mom and Dad often brought home doggie bags of leftovers when they ate out. In fact, they even ordered items from the restaurant menu specifically with us in mind. Needless to say, in our house, food crumbs in bed did not have time to get moldy.

Oh yeh, the forest had lots of edible games, and between Loki and Foxy, we didn't lack for hunting skills; I'll leave the rest to your imagination. The point being, the Lord helped those who helped themselves. We did not go hungry.

I would be prevaricating if I said we didn't contest against each other for food. As a rule, Mom and Dad nipped the problem at the bud when they made us "sit and stay" before they passed out our meals, and it was even distribution to all. I must declare that even distribution did not mean equal distribution. In this case, size mattered. The bigger you were translated to more food at dinner time. However, after they handed out food, Mom and Dad left it up to us for final disposition of the digestible. Each person ate from his or her own bowl; a nasal snort from Dad always ended any attempt at food fights. As I mentioned before, sometimes Loki went on the rag and did her domination routine, but mostly we were able to eat in peace.

Usually, everyone knew his or her place within the pack; however, Foxy did not appreciate being on the bottom rung of the ladder, thus sometimes created problems. I dealt with her aggression via direct action. More specifically, when she tried to get my goodies, I would just leap on top of her and smothered her with my body; that always forced her to whimper, as she signaled her surrender and the end of the contest. Taz, being quick on his paws, used his speed to achieve the same end. He simply reached out and shoved Foxy into the ground with his right front paw, and that was the end of that food fight.

As for Taz and me, we quickly reached an understanding, when he realized that his speed meant little against somebody twice his size and weight. All I had to do was to hold my ground over the food. In this case, the best offense was a good defense; let the other side run around and tire himself out, while you cut off his access to food supplies. It was a version of the Fabian Strategy, used most effectively by the famous Roman general <u>Quintus Fabius Maximus Verrucosus</u> to defeat Hannibal; another lesson I learned from Dad, our resident military historian.

CHAPTER 8

. . . The Shadow Knows

Self portrait

T he benefit of being the narrator of a book was that you got to devote a whole chapter of the material to yourself. As for the title of this chapter, well for those people who didn't know what it meant, do search the internet under "The Shadow Knows" and you will find out, ☺.

My birth mother was a Labrador Retriever and my sire was a Rottweiler. In terms of looks, I favored my lab ancestry—pure black stiff fur with webbed feet, and I weigh-in at 120 pounds with not an ounce of fat; however, dark splotches on my tongue gave evidence to my paternal genes.

Mom and dad adopted me when I was eight weeks old; and boy was I glad they picked me instead of one of my brothers or sisters. You see, I was the youngest of a brood of eight. Every one picked on me. I never got enough to eat. Oh yea, there was usually a lot of food for me in the bowl, a big empty lot. My siblings' idea of fun and games were "get the runt," guess who got to be the toy? Which meant I played a lot of hide and seek, I hid and they seeked. And that was why I was so happy when mom and dad came and got me when they did. They found "a cute ball of curly black fur" (their words) hidden under the porch steps.

At first, I was afraid of mom and dad; but they soon set my mind at ease. Mom held me in her lap and crooned to me gently, while stroking my body, as dad drove us to my new home. Wow, what a home—42 plus acres of trees, pond, creek, plus loads of critters to chase after, and no one to bully me, at least not in the house.

That evening, I had the first good meal of my life. All that food, with no competition in sight; I ate so much that my tummy was dragging on the floor. Wouldn't you know it; ten minutes after I finished eating, I threw them all back out. It seemed my digestive system just was not used to so much food at once. Nevertheless, I helped Mom clean up the mess I made.

I thrived in my new home and grew into a regular happy go lucky canine that got along well with most everybody. I loved my pack mates, swam in the pond, chased wild animals through the woods, and enjoyed full body massages. On the serious side, I considered protecting my home and the pack as an important responsibility. No stranger got near the house without my knowledge. My sharp ears could pick up strange noises from far, far away. So, don't even think about entering the house without my permission. I knew some people called me Cujo behind my back. But I didn't mind; it meant I had a reputation that made people think twice or thrice before they tried anything funny with our pack. As a famous military strategist said, "The best victory is the one you win without a fight." Guess from whom did I get that adage?

Although I tended to be suspicious of strangers, I was a pushover for kids. I just loved to play with children.

Best friends

Puppy love

They used me as a horse, a pillow and a toy. I took them for walks in the woods. However, I got antsy when they went near the pond or the swimming pool, for fear that they could drown. I tried to keep them from swimming, and had been known to clamp my teeth on the swimsuit of kids and pull them back from the edge of the water. But, kids would be kids, they always sneaked back into the water which forced me to jump in and swam in circles around them to prevent them from going under. Of course, Mom and Dad always rewarded me with yummy treats for my diligence in protecting the kids.

Kimberly was my best friend. We played in the woods together, and worked up a routine at Pets Only to entertain the guests. During some evenings, Gracie would kick off the show with a loud whistle followed by two bars from "When the Saints Come Marching In" to get everyone's attention. Kimberly then walked in with me at her heel, sans leash. Then, with the use of hand signals only, she had me "stop," "stay," "heel," "lay down," and "come" to her. Finally, she gave another "stay" command, then went over to the bar and picked-up a pot sticker from a plate that Dad had prepared and set aside for her. With a pot sticker in hand, she'd returned to place the tasty morsel atop the tip of my nose. Naturally, the aroma stimulated my nostrils, and opened the floodgate of saliva while I held steady and balanced the dumpling in place. Let me tell you, it was no easy task, resisting the urge to snap and swallow that delicious morsel. In no time, a torrent of drool flowed down my jaw, and created a large puddle between my paws, only then did she snap her fingers, which was the signal for me to flip the pot sticker high into the air and let it fall into my gullet on the way down. Of course, a chorus of cheers and applause followed for the "Lady and the Beast." Afterwards, Mom finished the act with a quick rendition of the "mop up."

*   *   *

Five dogs and three cats constituted an efficient mess making machine. Mom often griped about having to pick up after us, such as sofa pillows, toys, food bowls, leftover chew bones . . . etc. I pled guilty to those charges, but nobody ever taught me to clean house. Anyway, Mom initially used a laundry basket as our toy chest; but no sooner had she gathered them into the basket, before we swiped them back out to play. So she escalated the situation by using a cloth container with a zippered flap to store the toys. She thought that would take care of the toy control problem, but she underestimated me. I was tall enough to reach the top of the container, so all I had to do was tug on the zipper with my teeth to open a gap then knocked the container over, and the rest was history. Score one point for the pets.

$*$　　　　　$*$　　　　　$*$

Everybody knew that Labs were hunters. We had speed, a sharp sense of smell, keen hearing and excellent eyesight. I loved to run through the woods to discover the sources of different scents. I especially enjoyed darting about under the moonlit night, for you never know what you might come across.

One night, during the Fall hunting season, I came across a fresh deer leg and brought it home. Late into the night, a blood curdling scream roused everyone off the bed; lights flicked on and we saw Mom sat up in bed with my deer leg on the bedspread, next to her. *Oops, so that was where I had mislaid the find.* Without a word, Dad calmly looked around then reached over to run his hand over our heads. At length, he grabbed my right front paw; as I was the only one with damp cold fur and wet paws I guess I was caught wet-pawed.

He gingerly picked up the deer leg by the rubbery hoof and took it to the kitchen; all the while mumbled something about the "God Father" and some horse's head. I was disappointed that he did not praise me for such a unique find and I became really crestfallen when I followed him into the kitchen and saw him toss the leg good venison into the trash bin. I had my heart so set on having grilled leg of venison for breakfast.

The next night, I went hunting again and came back with another leg. To make the long story short, it ended up in the same waste can, and afterwards Dad locked the doggie door every evening, until the hunting season was over. So that ended my nightly romps, for a while, at the least.

*   *   *

Believe it or not, as the senior and the biggest male of the pack, I was much desired by the opposite sex. However, there had been a slight problem which I shall discuss at another time. But, I digress. As I had previously stated, Foxy was a beautiful and intelligent lady. When she achieved puberty, Taz started following her around and sniffing up her butt. However, the lady had set her heart on "Tall, Dark and Handsome" which created a comical situation. Regularly, after she had rejected Taz's advances, Foxy would run to me and smack me across the face with her backside. One day, after another round of face slapping, Mom and Dad took Foxy out for a ride, and we did not see Foxy for an entire day. When she finally came home, she looked sick and behaved

. . . The Shadow Knows

testy and irritable. A week passed before she recovered her spirit, but she no longer became an item of interest to Taz. Poor girl, I knew exactly how she felt and deeply sympathized with her condition.

CHAPTER 9

The Lady and the Tramp

Lady

Tramp

I leave you to guess, between Taz and Foxy, who was the Lady and who was the Tramp. Smirk, smirk. They were playmates from puppyhood. Mom picked Taz out of a litter of Boxers in which he was the only brindle. Foxy was a gift/rescue. She used to belong to Hassan, the Lebanese chef of the Inn. She proved to be too flighty, meaning she often took off running at the first opportunity. Hassan got tired of chasing after a dog until the dog decided to be caught. When Dad heard that Foxy was headed for the pound, he intervened and brought her home.

Now Dad also had some problems handling Foxy. She would run away at the first opportunity, but the wide expanse of the forty acres of woods helped contain the runaway and keep her out of harm's way. Also, Dad realized that Foxy liked to be with me, so whenever Foxy went AWOL, Dad would send me to bring her back. Needless to say, I always got my dog, gruff, gruff.

Coincidentally, her hunting skills quickly endeared her to Dad as she eradicated the rodents from the grounds around the house. So Dad tolerated her occasional straying. Eventually, Dad's patience and experience paid off, as Foxy learned the pack etiquette and settled into her proper role within the family.

Interestingly, for a dog, Foxy was extremely sensitive; her feelings could be easily bruised, and required immediate resolution. For instance, a scolding from Mom or Dad would cause her to mope and pout, with her tail dragging behind her until they gave in to her by talking gently and petting her.

You could tell she forgave them when her tail sprung back into a coil and she started strutting like she owned Mom and Dad.

Foxy was also very excitable, and when she got excited she 'tinkled.' Every time Becky (Hassan's wife and Foxy's original owner) visited us Foxy would jump excitedly and tinkle. That was one bad behavior that Dad could never get Foxy to change. Like I said, she was hard headed. Perhaps Dad should call Cesar Millan for help. You probably guessed by now that "The Dog Whisperer" was the favorite program within our pack.

In my humble opinion, Foxy was the least obedient dog of the pack. She required a leash for any activity outside of our home. Temperamental to the T, she'd snap and growl at the drop of a paw. I had never met anyone as bitchy as she was. How come Loki and Sheba were not like that? On the other paw, she was very observant, able to learn from other people's mistakes. For example, when we went on walks, sometimes Dad would order us to "heel," which meant we had to walk beside him or behind him. Often Taz, the eager beaver that he was, trotted ahead of the pack, thus received a tap on his posterior from Dad's boot for his troubles. Of course Taz quickly backed up to his trail position. After noticing this butt correction measure, Foxy immediately reined in her hunting instincts and walk beside Dad like a prim and proper lady.

Foxy Lady was true to her namesake of the wily fox when it came to social behavior. She felt her intelligence and her looks set her above the other members of the pack, except for

THE LADY AND THE TRAMP

Mom, Dad and Loki of course. As I mentioned before, she routinely bolted away from the house, which forced me to chase after her and fetch her home. At home, she 'beaugarded' Mom and Dad; when the other dogs came near Mom and Dad, she'd growl to establish her claim, sometimes even at Loki. No amount of admonishment from Mom and Dad could change her abrasive personality.

Interestingly, at meal time, the lady displayed an utter lack of social etiquette; she belched loudly after every meal. I thought only Arabs did that, not the Japanese. Her burp was so loud that I heard them from the next room; definitely not a very proper ladylike behavior.

*   *   *

Taz was almost the exact opposite of Foxy in terms of character. His happy go lucky personality made it nearly impossible to dampen his sanguine spirit. He was also a prankster, as attested by his aforementioned encounters with Bubba and Oscar. He loved to romp in the woods and tease the neighborhood dogs. His favorite victims were a pair of German Shepherds that we named Ashley and Thelma, because their weak barks sounded like they had "asthma." I must say they were a sad pair; their owner kept them behind a small fenced yard. They never got to go out and socialized with people. So they were naturally aggressive toward other dogs that passed nearby. Taz always ran up to them and hopped around to make friends, which drove the Shepherds into a frenzy of wheezing barks. For the first few times, I thought Ashley and Thelma would go into catatonic seizures and pass out from the excitement. After a while, it became a ritual game for Taz, to tease the pair of Shepherds.

However, in all fairness, I will have you know that Taz was well trained, as attested by the fact that Mom and Dad always took him for walks without a leash. Once, Taz joined a bunch of neighborhood canines in running after a bitch in heat. Dad decided Taz was still too immature to start a family, so he gave a sharp whistle then called aloud "Taz! Come!" Everyone at the Inn, including Dad, was surprised when Taz broke away from the running pack and ran back into the Inn. Suddenly, all the patrons at Pets Only burst out with a round of whistles, handclaps and paw stomping cheers. I didn't know whether they were cheering Dad's pet handling expertise or Taz's obedience, or perhaps both. Interestingly, Gracie chimed in with a bar from "Waltzing Matilda."

Taz was a free spirit who loved to go places. When you opened the front door, he would be out of the door before you could turn around. A natural hitchhiker, he liked cars, and it did not matter who was behind the wheel. When a car door was left open, he always jumped in without being told to do so. Often, after Mom and Dad had unloaded the car from a shopping trip, they invariably had to return to get the Spastic Kid out of the rear passenger seat. It became a routine for Mom and Dad to check the cars of visitors to ensure Taz did not went on another accidental joy ride.

The Lady and the Tramp

By the way, guess who was Rip's favorite dog? They matched each other's warped sense of humor and penchant for mischief. As the Chinese would say, they were like two skunks that reveled in each other's stench. They especially enjoyed each other's company during the winter months. With his high metabolic (warmth) rate and soft, velvety skin, Taz became an ideal ottoman. Rip liked to remove his shoes then placed his feet on Taz's body. It was a symbiotic relationship; Rip got a mobile foot warmer, in return Taz got a 'foot' massager.

CHAPTER 10

The Organ Harvesters

Now, we can't have a people story without a few words about the dreaded Veterinarians—the doctors. I am sure everyone had a horror story regarding those humans in long white coats. At first I did not mind them much. They were usually friendly and jovial, always tried to bribe you with cookies then groped you in your private body parts. I had wondered if you could charge them with being "petophiles." Of course, I would have nothing to do with them. I didn't like biscuits.

Then, on my first winter, when I was around six months old, I accidentally cut my right front paw on a jagged piece of ice in the woods. Mom tried to bandage up my wound, but the gauze and tape would never stay on my paw. I must admit, the fact that I often chewed at the itchy scabbed up area did not help the matter. Finally, Mom brought me to the Garrisonville Animal Hospital, and the Vet sewed me up. Unbeknownst to me, they tranquilized me and I awakened with major pains between my legs. When I bent over to check, I realized they had stolen my doghood. Needless to say, it was a traumatic experience, and ever since then I developed an extreme phobia of hospitals and clinics. The combined smell of antiseptics and medicine would send me into involuntary spasms.

In fact, for years, I would tremble whenever Mom or Dad made me get into the car for fear that they were taking me back to the organ harvesters. It was only after we moved to Florida, before I got over my 'automobile phobia;' but that's another story for another time. Meanwhile, my fear of the Vets left an indelible mark in my physic. You should know that I normally did not require a leash to go anywhere; I always followed Mom and Dad, and listen to their instructions impeccably. However, the leash became a necessity for visits to the Vets. On entering a clinic, my irrational fear took over; I lost total control of my bodily functions, and struggled to place Mom and Dad between me and the white coated ogre or ogress. It was scary and humiliating, but I just couldn't help it. As a preventive maintenance measure, Mom and Dad took to starving me and taking me for walks before going to the Vets; that was to have me empty my bowel before hand, so as to save them the expense of the clean up charges at the clinic.

I seriously believed they (the Vets) were in cahoots with the Aliens. You know, the ones that harvested organs of cattle and other animals. Or perhaps they collected and sold body parts like they did in China. Hey, that must have been it; didn't Dad say the Chinese ate everything that flied, except airplanes; and everything with four legs except tables.

I was not the only one to have suffered under the knife of the vets. Taz said he was born with a whip antenna like tail that was his pride and joy. Then one day, the vets went and chopped it to a stub. I wondered what they did with the dog's tail. Did they use it for research or food; I had heard ox tail soup was a delicacy, but dog tail soup? I don't know.

Sushi also had a bad experience with the vets. One day, she visited the vets and came home missing the claws from her front paws. It just befuddled me as to what would they (the vets) want with cats' claws. Perhaps for use as body jewelry such as necklace or ear rings?

Anyway, the mere thought of those organ harvesters still sent shivers from the point of my nose to the tip of my tail. All I had to say was keep your eyes open, your ears peeled and legs tightly clamped when you must visit a Veterinarian.

THE END

Epilogue

One cold winter, Loki and Sushi passed away within a month of each other. They were good friends and I was glad they had each other for company in Animal Heaven. I shall always miss Loki's loving green eyes and her wolfish smile. I was sorry to say, Sashimi took over Sushi's ambushing duties. Alas, as they say, there's no rest for the wicked.

As I previously mentioned, when the JJ's returned from their honeymoon, they not only left with their dogs and Pookie, but had they also took Auntie Sheba with them to San Jose. I believed that was someplace out west beyond Mom's hometown of Iowa. But, a year or so later, they moved down to sunny Orlando, Florida; however, without Auntie Sheba, for she had also gone to the Animal Heaven.

To get away from the cold winter and the memory of the lost companions, Dad took a job in Saint Petersburg, Florida, and we moved to that city. Consequently, I put to ink the final chapter for Pets Only.

Mom and Dad flew south and bought a house in Florida; in the process, they adopted a wild egret. I thought the bird might have been hired by the real estate agent to help sell the house. As Mom recalled, she was checking out the house, when the bird landed by the pool side of the house and escorted

Mom on her inspections of the property. Mom said that was the tipping point for the purchase of that house. Personally, I didn't like anybody that readily accepted friendly overtures from strangers; besides, that shameless bird's a cannibal. **She ate chicken!**

After they bought the house, Mom and Dad came home to settle the affairs in Virginia. Then, Dad and I drove down first to start on his job and got settled in the new home. It was three months before Mom joined us. She flew down to Tampa, and we met her at the airport. I didn't realize how much I missed her until when she got into the car; I leapt from the backseat onto her lap in the front seat. I was so happy that I talked and cried all the way home. I could tell she also missed me. She hugged and cried and kissed me and kept me (all one hundred and twenty pounds) in her lap for the entire trip.

The three of us, Taz, Foxy and I, voted on a group name—"The Three Dog Knights" to celebrate our new life in tropical Florida. It was a brand new smorgasbord of strange smells totally apart from the Virginia woodlands. We were in Heaven.

We got a swimming pool, a boat dock and all sorts of friendly furred, finned and feathered neighbors. Mom and Dad took us to people friendly parks, beaches and restaurants. We even got to order off the menu. We just loved it when they brought us food on our own plates. Maybe I could talk Dad into opening a franchise of the "Pets Only" at our new home.

Foxy Lady would have made a fantastic reception hostess. But, that's another story to be told at another time.

*   *   *

Author's Note: Each and every pet related incident described in this book were actual events that had taken place. Only the names, times and locations have been altered to protect the guilty. Any person that has interesting pet episodes and would like to have them included in the sequel to this book can send them to tanglongent@gmail.com, with "Pets" on the subject line. Contributor(s) will be cited in the credit line of the story.

Shadow Tang

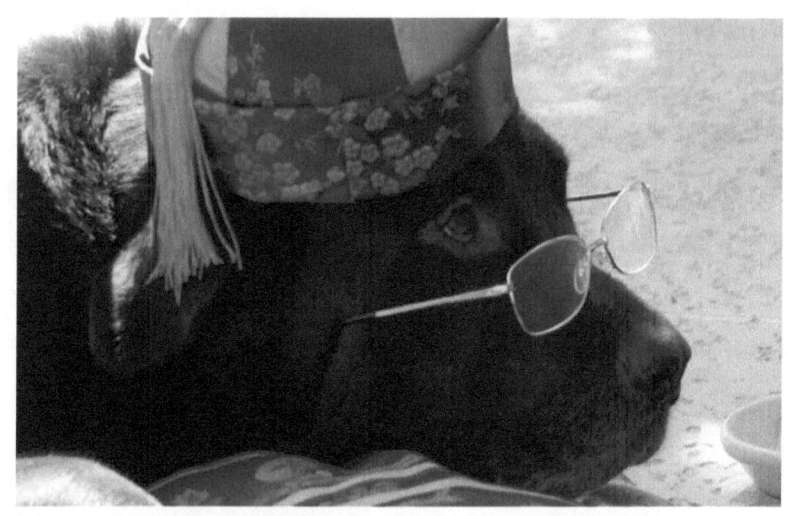

Shadow is a black Chesapeake Labrador Retriever.
He is intelligent, responsible and caring babysitter,
a gourmand and an exceptional guardian of the household.
He lives in Saint Petersburg, Florida with Taz,
Foxy Lady and Tang Long.

www.ingramcontent.com/pod-product-compliance
Lightning Source LLC
Chambersburg PA
CBHW031252280526
45784CB00004B/1822